Summary of

How to Raise an Adult
Break Free of the Overparenting Trap and Prepare Your Kid for Success

by Julie Lythcott-Haims

Instaread

Please Note

This is Key Takeaways, Analysis & Review.

Copyright © 2015 by Instaread. All rights reserved worldwide. No part of this publication may be reproduced or transmitted in any form without the prior written consent of the publisher.

Limit of Liability/Disclaimer of Warranty: The publisher and author make no representations or warranties with respect to the accuracy or completeness of these contents and disclaim all warranties such as warranties of fitness for a particular purpose. The author or publisher is not liable for any damages whatsoever. The fact that an individual or organization is referred to in this document as a citation or source of information does not imply that the author or publisher endorses the information that the individual or organization provided. This concise summary is unofficial and is not authorized, approved, licensed, or endorsed by the original book's author or publisher.

Table of Contents

Overview 4

Important People 6

Key Takeaways 8

Analysis 11

Key Takeaway 1 11

Key Takeaway 2 13

Key Takeaway 3 15

Key Takeaway 4 17

Key Takeaway 5 19

Key Takeaway 6 21

Key Takeaway 7 23

Key Takeaway 8 25

Key Takeaway 9 27

Author's Style 29

Author's Perspective 31

References 33

Overview

How to Raise an Adult: Break Free of the Overparenting Trap and Prepare Your Kid for Success is a book of parenting advice. The author, Julie Lythcott-Haims, is a former freshman dean at Stanford University and the mother of two teenagers.

While at Stanford University, Lythcott-Haims noticed that her students lacked life skills. They could not care for themselves, they had no grit, and they did not know what they wanted to be or how to be an adult. She saw parents accompanying students on campus, doing their work for them, and applying for jobs on their behalf. Lythcott-Haims concluded that parents, in an attempt to give their children every opportunity and help them get into the best school, were overparenting to the degree that they were not raising independent adults.

Parents want to keep their children safe, and provide opportunities. They want them to go to the best colleges. Top universities today are very competitive and the economy presents challenges. To ensure success, parents overparent, creating a family dynamic that results in stressed children who do not have the skills to get through life and are very anxious, as well as stressed parents who do not have lives of their own. By changing the way parents' raise their children, as well as changing ideas of success and the college process, parents can push back against the tide of overparenting and save themselves and their children.

Important People

Julie Lythcott-Haims: Julie Lythcott-Haims is a former dean of Stanford University, and a graduate of Stanford and Harvard Law School. She lives in Palo Alto, California, with her husband and two teenage children.

Sawyer: Sawyer is Lythcott-Haims's son, who was treated for Attention Deficit Hyperactive Disorder (ADHD). He is used in this book frequently as an example of Lythcott-Haims's experience as a parent in Palo Alto with a millennial child.

Avery: Avery is Lythcott-Haims's daughter.

Rachel: Rachel is a young woman from a wealthy Conservative Jewish family in Los Angeles whose parents did everything for her. She is an example of a child whose overparenting set her on the path to addiction.

Lawrence "Larry" Momo: Lawrence Momo is the director of college counseling at the preparatory school Trinity in New York and the former admissions dean at Columbia University. Like many others, he believes that the system of college applications and standardized testing is broken.

Bill Deresiewicz: Deresiewicz is the author of *Excellent Sheep: The Miseducation of the American Elite and the Way to a Meaningful Life*, a book about how learning and happiness are sacrificed to create students at elite schools.

Key Takeaways

1. Baby boomers grew up in a time of unprecedented success. They want to give their children opportunities and counter the way they were parented, but times have changed.
2. The world is not as unsafe as it seems, but society operates as though there are dangers to children waiting around every corner.
3. Childhood has become very scheduled in order for a child to succeed on a very limited path that negatively impacts a child's development. Children need unstructured time to grow, learn, and think for themselves.
4. Children learn through failure, responsibility, and mastery. When parents do everything for their children, they deny children the upside of failure and the ability to develop grit.
5. The college process is rigged in a way that creates undue stress and unrealistic expectations about the right schools. Parents must have a wider mindset about colleges.
6. Children who are overparented are completely unprepared for the challenges and

responsibilities of the job market and living alone. Parents need to teach independence.

7. Parents should strive for the authoritative parenting style instead of the authoritarian and permissive/indulgent styles common in millennial households.

8. The immense pressure young people face has led to the rise of study drugs.

9. Parents must let go of their egos and back off from their children. They can be better parents by reclaiming themselves and by being the people they want to be.

We hope you are enjoying this Instaread book

Download the Instaread mobile app to get unlimited text & audio summaries of bestselling books.

Visit instaread.co
to learn more.

Analysis

Key Takeaway 1

Baby boomers grew up in a time of unprecedented success. They want to give their children opportunities and counter the way they were parented, but times have changed.

Analysis

Baby boomers, the generation born after World War II, grew up often as latch-key kids to laissez-faire parents. When they came of age, they were beneficiaries of a booming economy that allowed them to do better than their parents. However, Millennials, or people between the ages of 18 and 34 in 2015, have more competition when applying to elite colleges and, after college, face an uncertain job market. To overcompensate for the way they were parented, and in an attempt to ensure their children's success, boomers tend to overparent. They assume that their children need to compete with other children to succeed.

There is a lot of evidence of the less stable times that today's children are growing up in. The millennial generation is the first generation in US history to be worse off than their parents' generation. According to a Pew Research study, this is because they are often saddled with student debt. Thirty-seven percent of US households with adults under 40 have student debt. Those with student loans have a net worth of $8,700 compared to $64,700 for those without student debt. These people are also less likely to own a home. According to a study by the National Association of Realtors, fewer than 25 percent of 30 year olds are home owners, as compared to 80 percent of baby boomers [1]. This disparity causes anxiety in parents, who want to ensure the best for their children and see only very set pathways to ensure this success.

Key Takeaway 2

The world is not as unsafe as it seems, but society operates as though there are dangers to children waiting around every corner.

Analysis

AMBER Alerts, milk cartons covered in faces of kidnapped children, and the 24-hour news cycle all give the impression that it is unsafe for children to be left alone. In today's world, parents who allow their children to walk home or play outside alone are vilified and, in extreme cases, suffer legal consequences. In reality the world is not that unsafe.

In fact, children today are much safer than they have ever been. Child victimization rates have plummeted dramatically since the 1970s. Between 1970 and 2009 sexual abuse has decreased by 52 percent, physical abuse by 53 percent, and bullying numbers have dropped by a third. Kidnapping, which still grabs headlines that make people think it is very common, is unlikely. The odds of a child today being murdered and kidnapped stand at 1.5 million to one [2]. Still, so called 'free range parents' face police investigations for letting their children play in the park or walk home alone. The Meitiv family in Maryland have been under investigation twice for allowing their children to wander from home without supervision [3]. However, keeping children so sheltered will prevent them from developing street smarts, making it less safe for them to be out in the world.

Key Takeaway 3

Childhood has become very scheduled in order for a child to succeed on a very limited path that can negatively impact a child's development. Children need unstructured time to grow, learn, and think for themselves.

Analysis

Parents are anxious to give children the skills they need to succeed and make sure they get into the right college. As a result, over-scheduling starts as early as preschool, with after-school activities, sports, hours of homework, and no time to daydream. Children today lack unstructured play time, something that is negative for their development and the family dynamic.

People seem to think that rushing around to different activities will create more successful children. But economists have found this is not the case. Steven D. Levitt of the University of Chicago studied this with another economist. They could find no evidence that parental choices correlated with academic success. In an interview, Levitt said: "...when it comes to the happiness of kids, that kind of cramming has got to be negatively correlated. Being rushed from one event to the other is just not the way most kids want to live their lives, at least not my kid [4]."

There is evidence that unstructured playtime is very important for growth. The American Academy of Pediatrics issued a report in support of unstructured play time. They found play to be essential in children reaching developmental milestones [5].

Key Takeaway 4

Children learn through failure, responsibility, and mastery. When parents do everything for their children, they deny children the upside of failure and the ability to develop grit.

Analysis

In today's culture, children grow up without failure. It is the era of participation prizes and of parents interfering in everything, including contesting a bad grade on behalf of a student and writing college applications for their children. Because of this, children lack valuable skills. They also have have a horrible experience when they fail as adults.

A recent book, *The Gift of Failure* by Jessica Lahey, tackles this issue head on. Lahey, who is a middle school teacher, asks parents to let their children fail, stating that if they do not, they will suffer great consequences. They will be unprepared when "failures that happen out there, in the real world, carry far higher stakes. [6]" She pushes back against the parents who do everything for their children, saying that their intervention undermines a child's confidence and education. They are failure deprived and not ready for the challenges of the world . In contrast, grit, the idea of showing up day after day and realizing that setbacks happen and success only comes with hard work, is one of the most important predictors of success. A study of contestants at the Scripps National Spelling Bee found that grit led to deliberate practice and spelling success [7]. Children need to be allowed to fail so they can develop grit and succeed on their own.

Key Takeaway 5

The college process is rigged in a way that creates undue stress and unrealistic expectations about the right schools. Parents must have a wider mindset about colleges.

Analysis

Parents want children to have the best chance of success. Most feel their children have to attend one of a handful of elite colleges, especially if they went to one themselves. They spend thousands on test prep and college counseling. But the widening applicant pool, along with the fact that students are applying to more colleges, makes a student's chance of getting into one akin to winning a lottery. For example, the 2014 admissions rate at Stanford University was 5.1 percent [8].

The admissions rate at elite universities is dropping for a variety of reasons. Colleges know they are measured partly in terms of their admissions rate, so they send mailers and advertise to try to get more people to apply. Because of the rise of the Common Application, and the amount of information about schools online, it is easier to apply to more schools, so students often expand their range. Also, it is a vicious cycle: as acceptance rates drop, students feel they need to apply to more schools to ensure they get in somewhere [9].

But parents need to let go of the mindset that if their child does not go to one of these elite colleges they will not be successful. Research shows that students who were accepted to elite schools, but then went elsewhere, were just as successful as those who attended elite schools. Just as many Fulbright Scholarships were awarded to students in 2014-2015 who attended the University of North Texas as those who attended the University of Michigan [10]. Families are spending time and money, as well as sacrificing their sanity, trying to get their children into elite schools. But it is not necessary for children to thrive.

Key Takeaway 6

Children who are overparented are completely unprepared for the challenges and responsibilities of the job market and living alone. Parents need to teach independence.

Analysis

Imagine the first week of college. A student needs to do laundry, but has never done it before. The student experiences huge amounts of stress as a result.

Many parents do not make their children do chores because they want to shield them from the unpleasant aspects of life, and they want their children to focus on their schoolwork and extracurriculars. But chores go a long way in terms of fostering self reliance and responsibility. Marilyn Rossman, a professor of family education at the University of Minnesota, studied 25 years of family data. She found that the best indicator of individuals' success during adulthood was whether as children they participated in household tasks. Rossman advises that parents model the tasks and start simple. It is also important to start early. It is much easier to introduce the idea of helping to a receptive four-year-old than a teenager. Chores teach children empathy, how to care for themselves, and how to contribute. These are all important skills that children who are only asked to focus on their schoolwork and extracurriculars miss out on [11].

Key Takeaway 7

Parents should strive for the authoritative parenting style, instead of the authoritarian and permissive/indulgent styles common in millennial households.

Analysis

There are two common parenting styles at play today that are detrimental to children. The first is authoritarian, where the parents set strict rules and are cold. This style is exemplified by Amy Chua's popular book *Battle Hymn of the Tiger Mother*. The other style, permissive/indulgent, is very common in millennial/boomer households. The parents live to serve the children and give in to their every whim. A combined style, authoritative, which mixes both warmth and freedom with rules and responsibility, has the best outcome.

Research suggests that the authoritative parenting style has many upsides. Children raised in this context are more likely to become independent, self-reliant, well-liked, well-behaved, as well as emotionally and academically successful. They are also less likely to have problems, such as anxiety, depression, and drug use. Research shows that having even one parent in a household who parents in this style can have good and lasting effects on children. Despite cultural differences in child-rearing styles, authoritative parenting can work in different countries and cultural contexts. Although in different countries this style is more or less democratic, where parents are more or less likely to take their children's point of view into account when making decisions, authoritative parents reason with their children. They promote inductive discipline, which helps children become more empathetic and kind [12]. Although it is tempting to give in to other parenting styles, especially the very common permissive style, when parents use the authoritative style they are actually setting up their children for success.

Key Takeaway 8

The immense pressure young people face has led to the rise of study drugs.

Analysis

As an example of how pernicious the use of so called study drugs, or drugs that help a student study better, can be, Lythcott-Haims details a time when she considered using them for her son, Sawyer, who has ADHD, in order to give him an advantage in finishing his homework. As academic pressures increase and students do not want to be denied the advantage of all of their classmates, the use of study aid drugs increases as well. But the long-term effects are not known.

According to the Centers for Disease Control (CDC), 19 percent of boys aged 14 to 17 have been diagnosed with ADHD and 10 percent are taking medicine for it. Ten percent of girls have been diagnosed. The CDC estimates a 53 percent increase in diagnosis over the last decade. These numbers have caused doctors to sound the alarm on over-diagnosis and the misuse of Ritalin. Dr. William Graf, a pediatric neurologist at Yale, told

The New York Times that diagnosis was going into the realm of 'pure enhancement' to students who were actually healthy [13]. The easy access to these drugs on a high school and college level can, like other aspects of the parental arms race, make parents and students want to use drugs just to get up to the level of other students. It is another aspect of this problematic theory that everything has to be done to get ahead.

Key Takeaway 9

Parents must let go of their egos and back off from their children. They can be better parents by reclaiming themselves and by being the people they want to be.

Analysis

A lot of the problems in overparenting are tied up in ego. Parents are competing with other parents and care what other people think. In this way, they use their children to judge themselves. But instead of living vicariously through their children, parents achieve better families and more parental happiness when they model success.

An important and often neglected part of parenting is self-care. Although the temptation is to neglect it, if parents want to be as happy as their children and be better parents, they need to care for themselves. Laura Markham, Ph.D., puts forth the idea of radical self care as a parenting solution in *Psychology Today*. She advises parents to nurture themselves as they would their children, giving themselves time off and breaks. She advises parents to make time for exercise and to work hard to manage their stress. Perhaps most important, she tells parents to make sure they take responsibility for their own lives and problems and not put off joy [14]. Parents need to be the change they want to be. By starting with self care, parents are both modeling a way to live for their children and parenting them better than when they are hyperfocused on their child's success and slaves to their every want.

Author's Style

Lythcott-Haims writes in an easy to comprehend style. She combines many different techniques in her book. She uses personal anecdotes about raising her children, Sawyer and Avery, in order to show her own thought process as a parent, that she is human, and that she is guilty of the same sins as other parents. She uses the testimony of other children, such as Rachel who ended up in Beit T'Shuvah, an addiction treatment center, as well as many anecdotes from her time as dean. She also utilizes the expertise of professionals in the field, such as Larry Momo, a former admissions dean at Columbia University, and many important books related to the problem, such as William Deresiewicz's *Excellent Sheep: The Miseducation of the American Elite and the Way to a Meaningful Life*.

Lythcott-Haims switches between a more narrative, argued approach that consolidates all of the different types of research she has done, and explicit directives to parents about how to parent better and teach certain behaviors. As a result, it is interesting to read for both a lay reader interested in parenting in the US, and a parent looking to solve specific problems and stop overparenting.

Author's Perspective

Lythcott-Haims began to notice the problems she outlines in the book during her her job as a dean at Stanford University and in her experience raising children in Palo Alto in Silicon Valley. She also attended elite universities as a student. Because of this, she focuses on overparenting as an epidemic affecting a specific group of people. As she acknowledges, many of the conclusions she comes to would be different in the study of different socioeconomic groups. It still makes for a fascinating study.

~~~~~~~ END OF INSTAREAD~~~~~~~

Thank you for purchasing this Instaread book

Download the Instaread mobile app to get unlimited text & audio summaries of bestselling books.

Visit instaread.co
to learn more.

References

[1] Sightings, Tom. "8 Differences Between Boomers and Millennials." *U.S. News & World Report*, accessed October 28th, 2015. http://money.usnews.com/money/blogs/on-retirement/2014/05/20/8-differences-between-boomers-and-millennials

[2] Villano, David. "The Kids Really Are All Right." *Pacific Standard*, accessed October 28th, 2015. http://www.psmag.com/books-and-culture/the-kids-really-are-all-right-58651

[3] Wallace, Kelly. "Maryland Family Under Investigation Again for Letting Kids Play in Park Alone." *CNN*, accessed October 28th, 2015. http://www.cnn.com/2015/04/13/living/feat-maryland-free-range-parenting-family-under-investigation-again/

[4] Tugend, Alina. "Family Happiness and the Overbooked Child." *The New York Times*, accessed October 28th, 2015. http://www.nytimes.com/2011/08/13/your-money/childrens-activities-no-guarantee-of-later-success.html

[5] "New AAP Report Stresses Play for Healthy Development." *American Academy of Pediatrics*, accessed October 28th, 2015. http://www2.aap.org/pressroom/play-public.htm

[6] Lythcott-Haims, Julie. "'The Gift of Failure' by Jessica Lahey. *The New York Times*, accessed October 28th, 2015. http://www.nytimes.com/2015/08/23/books/review/the-gift-of-failure-by-jessica-lahey.html

[7] Lehrer, Jonah. "Which Traits Predict Success? (The Importance of Grit)." *WIRED*, accessed October 28th, 2015. http://www.wired.com/2011/03/what-is-success-true-grit/

[8] Snider, Susannah. "10 Colleges and Universities with the Most Competitive Admission Rates." *U.S. News & World Report*, accessed November 5th, 2015. http://news.yahoo.com/10-colleges-universities-most-competitive-admissions-rates-140000679.html;_ylt=A0LEViWsgjtWSY8AhYMnnIlQ;_ylu=X3oDMTEzdGRpM2xwBGNvbG8DYmYxBHBvcwMxBHZ0aWQDRkZSQTAyXzEEc2VjA3Nj

[9] Perez-Pena, Richard. "Best, Brightest and Rejected: Elite Colleges Turn Away Up to 95%."

The New York Times, accessed October 28th, 2015. http://www.nytimes.com/2014/04/09/us/led-by-stanfords-5-top-colleges-acceptance-rates-hit-new-lows.html

[10] Kretzschmar, Michelle. "What Happens to People Who Go to Colleges No One Has Ever Heard Of?" *DIY College Rankings*, accessed October 28th, 2015. http://diycollegerankings.com/what-happens-to-people-who-go-to-colleges-no-one-has-ever-heard-of/5240/

[11] Wolf, Liz. "The Value of Chores for Children." *Parenthood.com*, accessed October 28th, 2015. http://www.parenthood.com/article/the_value_of_chores_for_children.html#.VjEZNWTBzGc

[12] Dewar, Gwen. "The Authoritative Parenting Style: Warmth, Rationality and High Standards." *Parenting Science*, accessed October 28th, 2015. http://www.parentingscience.com/authoritative-parenting-style.html

[13] Kant, Garth. "Radical Increase in Kids Prescribed Ritalin." *WND*, accessed October 28th, 2015. http://www.wnd.com/2013/04/radical-increase-in-kids-prescribed-ritalin/

[14] Markham, Laura. "Committing to Radical Self-Care." *Psychology Today*, accessed October 28th, 2015. https://www.psychologytoday.com/blog/peaceful-parents-happy-kids/201401/committing-radical-self-care